How To Be Owned By A

Simple Action Plan For First Time
Who Have NO Idea What They Are _____ ____

Kate C.

Legal & Disclaimer

The information contained in this book and its contents is not designed to replace nor take the place of any form of medical or professional advice; it is not meant to replace the need for independent medical, financial, legal or other professional advice or services, as may be required. The content and information in this book has been provided for educational and entertainment purposes only.

The content and information contained in this book has been compiled from sources deemed reliable, and it is accurate to the best of the Author's knowledge, information and belief. However, the Author cannot guarantee its accuracy and validity and cannot be held liable for any errors and/or omissions. Further, changes are periodically made to this book as and when needed. Where appropriate and/or necessary, you must consult a professional (including but not limited to your doctor, attorney, financial advisor or such other professional advisor) before using any of the suggested remedies, techniques, or information in this book.

Upon using the contents and information contained in this book, you agree to hold harmless the Author from and against any damages, costs, and expenses, including any legal fees potentially resulting from the application of any of the information provided by this book. This disclaimer applies to any loss, damages or injury caused by the use and application, whether directly or indirectly, of any advice or information presented, whether for breach of contract, tort, negligence, personal injury, criminal intent, or under any other cause of action.

You agree to accept all risks of using the information presented inside this book.

You agree that by continuing to read this book, where appropriate and/or necessary, you shall consult a professional (including but not limited to your doctor, attorney, or financial advisor or such other advisor as needed) before using any of the suggested remedies, techniques, or information in this book. While the book refers to real-life situations, the names mentioned may have been changed.

Cover Photo: Theodore
For SW & Julia...ditto

Table of Contents

Introduction

Are you thinking of getting a cat but feel unsure because you have zero or little experience with these adorable yet mystique felines? To make matter worse, you don't know any friends or family who are cat owners to ask for advice. You try to read and find out more on the internet but it is just way too much information for you to digest. Instead you end up watching funny, cute cat videos on YouTube and imagine what your life will be like with a cat.

But there is a better way!

In this book, you will be shown the A to Z of having a cat. You will know right from the beginning what to prepare and expect even before your first cat's homecoming. You'll learn about cat-proofing your house, communication tips, training, diet and so much more.

For most of my life I've been fond of animals and always wanted to adopt a pet. When I finally got my own home, I made good on my promise but it took me one year to feel ready. Because all my friends, family and neighbors are dog owners, I had no one to guide me. Ironically, I became the first and only cat owner in my circle and showed others that cats can also be as affectionate and expressive as their beloved dogs.

Whatever doubts and questions you have about getting a cat, you will benefit from the simple-to-follow action plan in this book which acts like a map to help you and kitty make a smooth transition together with less hiccups.

The book you are about to read is not written by some cat expert or cat fancier but once-upon-a-time virgin cat owner like yourself. What I learned from my experience and that of others is that it is a fine line that separates those of us who are struggling, overwhelmed cat owners from those who are prepared and informed.

After reading this book, you'll transform yourself from a newbie to a cat-whisperer. Others will be wondering how you did it in so little time. As a bonus you'll end up having more time and energy to bond with your new kitty.

Take action now and transform yourself into a smart kitty owner!

Scroll up to the top and Click Buy Now.

Disclaimer: This book is written from the perspective of a first-time cat owner who does not claim to be a cat expert in any way.

Chapter 1: Theodore

The commercial facility I was directed to, to meet my prospective cat, turned out to be a pet grooming shop with a dedicated adoption room. It was the most gorgeous adoption room I've ever seen. All the cats were free to roam around with lots of toys and even a manmade giant tree that they could climb and nap on. Meanwhile adopters could sit on kid-sized chairs while observing the cats' playground. Gwen, the cheery lady-boss-cum-fosterer apologized for being caffeine overdosed. She gave me a whirlwind crash course on cats before dropping Felix, a tuxedo kitten, onto my unsuspecting lap. Felix fidgeted and furred all over me (dark clothing was a bad idea) before deeming me boring and leaping off in a flash. I was overwhelmed but fascinated by all these feline activities around me. If this was a test-drive, what would a lifelong commitment be? Okay, instead of juggling ten to fifteen cats I'll just be dealing with ONE cat right? Totally doable for a virgin cat owner, right?

Whether you are a first time cat owner or just curious about these fascinating felines, you're about to be transformed into a cat-whisperer. Well, at least a theoretical one. Hands-on is of course another level that comes with experience.

I deliberated for one year before adopting my cat Theodore. When we met, I was attracted to this silver tabby's seemingly demure disposition. Of course, he turned into quite something else when he realized he was the "only child" in this household. His experienced fosterers were genuinely surprised at how he transformed into a little prima donna. Well, I don't think I spoilt him but then again, I had no idea what I was doing.

Being a first time cat owner, I had so many questions about caring for my cat. Theodore's fosterers were my only source of guidance and they were most helpful to guide me along the way. But since each cat's personality differs, it was pretty much trial and error - just like no two babies are alike.

In the beginning things were so bad that I scrutinized his adoption papers for the "return clause". But alas, there wasn't. So we remained stuck together hanging on by a thin thread.

I'll briefly describe Theodore to give you a fuller picture of what I was dealing with. He was found abandoned in a school with the possibility of being culled, before being rescued. Once home-sweet-home, he turned into a "talkative", vocal and demanding kitty. He stalked, jumped everywhere and broke several things. He meowed, yeowed hangrily (angry + hungry) round the clock. Basically he demanded food all the time like he was a growing adolescent. He was very different from my ideal of a quiet, self-sufficient and independent kitty companion. Instead I was overwhelmed by a constantly noisy, demanding and hungry cat who followed me everywhere. I couldn't work in peace or even go to the toilet without him following.

In time, I realized Theodore is just a very vocally expressive cat with a hearty appetite; most of the time he just meows for food, attention, boredom or playtime. I too, became more accommodating and flexible with his feeding. Basically, he will try to bargain dinner from 4pm, 4.01, 4.03... till I caved. Then an hour later, he'll feign amnesia and yeows for food again. This is basically our daily cycle / struggle.

One year later, I have grown to love this little expressive son of mine. He is not a lap cat and doesn't like to be cuddled too much. But we accept each other's space and differences. He often disturbs my work by laying across the keyboard or pinning the mouse underneath his body. Sometimes he'll insist on napping on my office chair while I take the stool. Right now, he has just been fed and is in a food coma, which buys me some time to speed type.

If you are considering having a cat, the golden rule is TIME. Give your new family member and yourself time to adjust. Teething and scratching hiccups are a given. But it will be worthwhile in the end, especially when you finally accept that a cat can't be trained in the conventional way. Instead you learn to flow with your cat's quirks. Trust me, your life will be easier too.

This book is basically written by a virgin cat owner who once had many, many questions like you. I truly hope reading this book will ease your journey and learning curve, so you won't take too long to bond with your cat.

"A journey of a thousand cats begins with one." - Meow Tze

Chapter 2: Basics - Before Home-Sweet-Home - Doing It Right First

"Well begun is half done" – Aristotle

1) Cat-Proofing Your House: Is your cat going to be an indoor or outdoor cat? High-rise or landed property? I live in a high-rise building, which means I had to cat-proof all windows and gates with mesh. There're several options such as fiberglass wires, PVC mesh, insect screen, hard plastic wire net, invisible grille - most can be found in your hardware store, either DIY or professionally if your budget permits. For DIY, my experience is to start with a small window first before doing bigger areas such as the gate. Mistakes will also be less obvious. Once you get the hang of it, the rest will be quite easy.

Note: If your cat is going to be an outdoor pet, you might want to install cat flaps beforehand.

Now that your house is escape-proof, it's time to cat-proof your furniture such as couch, beds, drapes, wallpaper or carpets which might be used for spontaneous "sharpening". For this, I bought anti-scratch tapes to paste on the sides of my couch and bed. Or you can also use regular double-sided tape or pets' anti-scratch sprays.

You might also want to install child-locks on certain cupboards or doors. Theodore knows how to "open sesame" my sliding wardrobe door by using his paws and snout. I've lost count how many times I caught him napping in a nest of my clean towels. Well, cats are resourceful and sneaky like that.

Home-Sweet-Home:

Now you are ready to bring kitty home-sweet-home. Remember everything is trial and error. Learn to be flexible like your cat. As prepared as you are, you'll probably still need to make some changes.

You know the saying "fickle feline" is really true. Cats are unpredictable and change their minds frequently. At first Theodore was uninterested in the open dustbins but soon discovered delicious leftover breads, so I had to change to heavy duty pedal bins. Initially he took no notice of my Yankee candle until one day he got bored and pushed it down. Now I hide all my candles away till I need them. One afternoon, he flooded my kitchen when he bit a few holes in the washing machine pipes to create a "fountain" for his amusement. His owner was not amused by her cat's antics.

Some people claim cats are generally smarter than dogs. But I suspect cat-owners are smarter because they have to constantly be one step ahead of their cats. After a while, I learned to anticipate his moves especially if he starts fixating on something e.g. he will stare at my glass cabinet as if mind-mapping how to ascend it (he gave up after launching at it a few times).

Tip: If you don't want your cat to fondle your holiday ornaments or family heirlooms - which of course they only go for the breakables and fragile - put them somewhere safe. This was the lesson I learned after a few breakages. You see, unlike Fido, kitty doesn't adhere to your rules. Save the heartaches and store your valuables away.

Lesson: Learn to flow with your cat instead of expecting your cat to conform. Life will be a lot easier with less breakage to clean up.

2) Food

Kibbles (dry food): Grain free vs Regular

Grain free refers to high protein and low carbohydrate diet.

The theory is grain free diet resembles cats' natural diet because they are carnivores. The advantages are higher amounts of protein using meat or fish, and less allergies triggered by grains. The disadvantages are higher fat content and more expensive.

I feed Theodore a grain free diet as this was recommended by his fosterers. After several months, his initial broom-like fur has turned very soft, probably due to a combination of quality food and regular grooming.

Do note, some so-called grain free products contain inappropriate carbohydrates such as rice, oatmeal, barley and corn. Look for protein as the No. 1 listed ingredient. The "First Mate" kibbles that Theodore eats has 92% or 95% protein from chicken or fish, with potatoes and blueberries as carbohydrates. "Sanabelle" no-grain poultry is also another brand he likes.

I'm thankful Theodore is not fussy with his food because the first time I made the mistake of buying a 10 lbs / 4.5kg bag (my kitty only weighed 8.4 lbs / 3.8kg then) which took forever to finish. Some picky eaters might only eat certain brands, so start small. Observe if your cat likes his food and has no side-effects such as diarrhea or vomiting.

Canned food (wet food)

As a rule of thumb, look for canned food that has less fillers and carbohydrates in the contents.

Theodore's highlight of the day is what I like to call his gourmet Japanese brand canned food "Aixia". He gets super excited and howls if I take too long to prepare dinner. This human grade canned food is so yummy that even his human finds it palatable. Two slices of bread with gourmet cat food plus mayo and ketchup makes a delicious sandwich, and you really can't tell the difference. I was sold immediately once I tasted a sample (of the canned food not the sandwich).

There are also some cat owners who advocate only wet food (more moisture) or raw food diet (raw meaty bone). This is an ongoing debate. Feel free to do further research and experiment what works best for you. Personally I chose the middle way and feed Theodore both dry and wet food.

Whatever you decide, provide the best quality food you can afford as an investment on your cat's wellbeing. Healthy cat equals happy cat.

How Much To Feed?

You can follow the recommended feeding guide on the food packaging. E.g. Theodore weighs 10.6 lbs / 4.8kg so it's 1/3 to 2/3 cup of kibbles or 5 to 8 tablespoons. I leave a measuring tablespoon in the container for convenience. But honestly, it's hard to keep track because he is such a snacker.

3) Solid Sisal Scratch Post

Rule of thumb: Choose a post that is taller than your kitty at full height with heavy base.

This scratch post is important because it will prevent your cat from scratching your furniture or wallpaper and it also helps to keep kitty's claws trimmed.

Get one that is tall and big enough for your cat to stretch out to the top on their hind legs while they scratch and not hunched over. Please make sure it is a good quality one with a solid and heavy base so it won't topple on your cat.

I introduced Theodore to his scratch post by rubbing some irresistible catnip on it. Now he has a habit of scratching it daily, especially when he wants to be praised. I also rotate the base weekly as he tends to only scratch the front part.

You can also get a fancy cat condo but make sure they are of good quality and won't topple on your cat.

4) Stainless steel, glass or ceramic food bowls

Stainless steel, glass or ceramic are all good but avoid plastics which contain BPA and other harmful toxic. I opted for stainless steel bowls because they are non-breakable and easy to clean. But do note some fussy cats do not like the taste of their food served in stainless steel.

5) Water Fountains or Drinking Bowls

Water fountains are costlier than your humble drinking bowls, but a worthwhile investment in your cat's long-term health. Many cats are notorious for not drinking frequently, which might cause kidney or bladder problems.

Theodore took to his bubbling fountain like a duck to water. It comes with a carbon filter that cleans and oxygenates water through bubbling action thus producing tastier water. Somehow the fountain effects make water so much more inviting to our cats. Cat logic?

I like it for several reasons:

- It doesn't spill or splash onto the floor even when Theodore is drinking.

- At 1.8L capacity, I don't need to change or add water daily.

- I don't have to worry about stagnant water attracting insects.

Cons:
- It needs electricity to operate 24/7.

- The filter, although inexpensive, has to be replaced every few months.

Do shop around as there are many different types, ranging from free-falling water flow, bubbling, whirlpool or 3-in-1 types.

Most cats are drawn to running water. Some even drink from a running faucet. So it also doubles as an entertainment for some cats.

6) Litter Box - Covered or Uncovered?

Cat litter boxes come either covered / hooded or uncovered. The covered types are really more for humans who don't want to see or smell their cats' business. Cats don't need privacy so it is really your call.

Theodore uses a covered box with removable hood and flap door as I didn't want to risk my clean laundry accidentally landing on it. But I removed the flap door to give him easier access and ventilation. A covered box also means there is less litter flying out when he uses it. He seems comfortable using a covered litter box but some cats might avoid it.

An uncovered box will have better ventilation and easier to clean without removing the hood. Otherwise consider one with high edges so that the cat litter won't fly out. Whichever you decide, it's important to get an adequate and spacious size for your cat. You don't want your cat to feel cramped and avoid using it.

7) Cat Litters

Types: Clumping, pine, recycled paper, silica gel crystals, corn, grass, clay, wheat etc.

There are numerous types of cat litter in the market. If your cat is already litter trained on a particular type, then stay with it unless it's not working out.

Here are some common ones:

Clumping Clay is made from bentonite and highly absorbent and turns into solid clumps when your cat urinates. Easy to scoop and clean. Economical.

Drawbacks: Dusty and non-biodegradable. Might stick to your cat's paws resulting in some messiness as he walks around.

Non-Clumping Clay is made from clay without bentonite. It absorbs urine but doesn't clump. Cheaper than clumping clay.
Drawbacks: Some moist litter left behind will start smelling soon and require frequent changing.

Note: Sodium bentonite might cause health related problems if swallowed or inhaled.

Silica Gel Crystals is like the desiccant found in our foods and medicine. It is highly absorbent, good odor control and almost dust-free.

Drawbacks: More expensive but long-lasting. Some cats don't like the sharp edged granules which can be dangerous if ingested in large quantity when they clean their feet.

Recycled Paper comes in pellets or granules. It is dust-free, highly absorbent and biodegradable. Only the granule type forms urine clumps.

Pine is natural and made of ecological sawdust that is decomposable and flushable. The pine scent acts as an effective odor control. The pellets are somewhat clumping and turns into sawdust which needs to be replaced regularly.

Drawbacks: Might need more cleaning and your cat might throw some particles out. Some cats might not like the pine smell.

Personally I didn't have to decide as Theodore was already litter-trained on pine by his tree hugging fosterers. I was extremely thankful he came to me already litter trained and we had no accidents.

My personal review of Pee Wee pine & EcoHus litter box:

Great odor control thanks to its pine scent, which is also acceptable to Mr. Theodore. I have no issues with the cleaning thanks to the "self-cleaning" Pee Wee litter box. It comes with a top tray with sieve that allows the soiled sawdust to disappear through its holes into the bottom tray. I will give the box a good shake so that more soiled sawdust will fall through. Besides disposing solid waste daily, I empty out the bottom tray on alternate days. I also line the bottom tray with pet pee pads aka pet diapers to collect all the fallen soiled sawdust which I can just wrap and dispose. I must give due credit to Theodore's genius fosterers who recommended the pee pads since they've an army to clean after.

If you are considering pine litter, it is much more convenient to get a litter box with a sieve. Otherwise all the soiled and clean pine will mix together, with nowhere to go until you manually sieve them apart.

Drawback: Self-cleaning boxes cost three to four times more than regular ones. Alternatively you can check YouTube on DIY sieve tray if you're handy with tools.

Some general considerations when choosing cat litter:

- Ease of cleaning

- Effectiveness

- Cost

- Odor control

- Absorbency

- Eco-friendly

- Flushable

- Non-toxic

Experiment and see what works for you. Lastly, cross your fingers kitty agrees with your choice of litter.

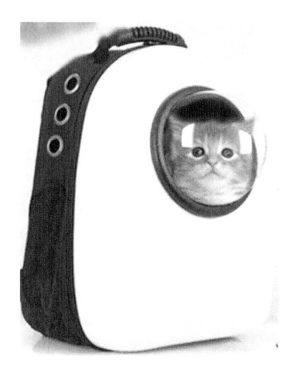

8) Carrier Bag - Transportation or Sightseeing?

A proper pet carrier is handy for a trip to the vet, pet sitter or groomer unless you want to use a makeshift box. It normally comes in canvas or plastic. There are special airline approved carriers or crates if you foresee traveling with your cat.

The latest trend is a cute backpack aka catpack which features a bubble window that "gives your cat a window to the world". Now your indoor cat can be a "cosmonaut" and come out for some scenery and fresh air in a cool designer catpack.

Looks aside, the most important thing is to make sure the carrier is hardy and escape-proof.

Personally I opted for a foldable heavy-duty canvas carrier as it's washable, takes up less space and can be stored away easily.

9) Mesh & Deterrents

Mesh: Strong polyester mesh, fiberglass wires, insect screen or hard plastic wire net which you can get from your DIY shop or online. There are also professional invisible window grilles or cat mesh installations. Window and gate mesh is a must for preventing falls and escapes especially for high-rise buildings.

Cat deterrents: Sticky tape, strips, double-sided tape or pet sprays for your furniture, carpet or wallpaper to prevent unwanted scratching. I had success with cat sticky tape on my couch and bed. You can also try Sticky Paws or similar products.

10) Toys

I was really excited when shopping for Theodore's first toys. There were so many toys at the pet shop, which will he fancy?

Theodore's Verdict:

Losers: Fancy wands, teasers, electronic motion toy, tunnels, battery-operated weasel etc. only held his attention for a minute. After plucking and tearing out all the feathers and furs (if any), they are now deemed passé to him. Only a featherless wobble toy survived his stringent testing.

Winners: Free shipping boxes, paper bags, ping pong balls, ribbons, more boxes, twist ties, drinking straws, paper clips, bottle caps, toothbrushes etc. Well, the magic number is anything less than $1 or FOC.

Lesson: I know it's hard but try not to overbuy. You can try making your own toys with boxes and clothes pegs. I once made him a tent out of cardboard, an old t-shirt and clothes hangers - he slept in it until he outgrew it. If you are in the mood, there are plenty of DIY cat toys on YouTube.

Recap: Resist overbuying. Buy or make some basics and see what floats his boat. Mine prefers big boxes to play hide and seek, ping pong balls (he can whack a mean game) and fancy long ribbons to pounce and chase like a snake. His latest muse is chasing metallic plastic twist ties - those you use for sealing bags and it costs less than $1 too.

11) Pet Monitor - IP Camera

If you are always away and your kitty is home alone, you might want to consider installing an IP camera. Somehow it gives me a peace of mind to be able to check on Theodore via my smartphone when I'm out the whole day.

12) How Much Is That Kitty In The Window? - Initial Investment & Recurring Expenses

Bringing home a pet is like having a baby. You need to be prepared for some initial investments and recurring expenses. Consider it an investment because by investing in quality stuff, you reap the benefits of a healthy and happy cat which means less visits to the vet.

Below is a list of general items in preparation of Theodore's arrival.

Initial Investment:

- 1 carton of wet food

- 1 bag of kibbles

- Pork liver treats

- Jerky fish treats

- Scratching post

- Cat litter box (covered type)

- Cat litter (pine wood)

- Pee pads (to line litter box)

- Catnip toy

- Stainless steel bowls

- Motorized drinking water fountain

- Collapsible carrier

- Grooming brush

- Cat collar

- ID Tag (engraved with owner's contact info)

- Window & gate mesh (to prevent cat escape)

Total: Approx US$500

Recurring Items:

- Wet food

- Kibbles

- Cat litter

- Rescue Remedy

- Treats

- *Optional grooming (bath + nail clipping)

Monthly: Approx US$70

Micro-chipping (one-time):

A microchip the size of a grain of rice is inserted under your cat's skin between his shoulder blades. When scanned it will identify your cat with a unique ID number linked to your contact details. This lifesaver is a simple and effective way to reunite you to your cat if he ever gets lost outside.

Note: Micro-chipping can be done at your vet. Or you can check with your local animal shelters or rescue groups which often do vaccinations and micro chipping for less. Also do remember to update any changes to your contact details in future.

Chapter 3: House Rules - Feeding Frequency, Restricted Zones and Sleeping Areas

1) Free Feeding Vs Scheduled Feeding

Free feeding means leaving food in the bowl for your cat, allowing him to eat as much as he chooses and when. The advantage is that when you're out the whole day, you don't have to rush home to feed your starving cat. Disadvantage is that your cat can become overweight especially if you use a food dispenser.

Scheduled feeding means controlled portions at fixed times. This is doable if you have a predictable schedule or work from home. This is also the healthier method, since you are limiting the food intake. This is the method I chose with Theodore whom I'm pleased to say is maintaining his svelte figure steadily at 10.6 lbs / 4.8kg.

In-between his meals, he also gets some special treats. These are normally single-ingredient, unflavored and human-grade freeze dried chicken, salmon or bonito treats. I tried them myself and even promoted these healthy snacks to my bemused guests. Thanks to these uber delicious treats, Theodore learned to do high-fives which is always a crowd pleaser and bragging rights for his mama.

2) Restricted Zones & Sleeping Rules

Many have forewarned that cats cannot be trained like dogs. But you can still lay down some basic guidelines. E.g. Is kitty going to sleep with you? Any restricted zones like closets, storeroom or baby room? Does kitty share human food? Free feeding or fixed meals?

Have a general consensus within the household beforehand, so that kitty will be less confused (or conniving). Also you don't want to find out kitty has been getting ice-cream on the sly from your housemate.

3) Privacy - What's That To Your Cat? -Nothing

When I adopted Theodore, I did not realize I was also relinquishing my privacy and personal space. Cats simply do not understand or care about the concept of personal space. Or maybe cats are communal creatures? Anyway, get used to "small brother" or sister watching your every move. In the beginning, I pretended I'm a somewhat famous celebrity being watched by the paparazzi or stalker - depending on my mood.

I don't know what is it with cats, but most have a deep dark fascination with bathrooms. Silver Shadow aka Theodore doesn't understand why he can't hang out there. Sometimes I see his furry white paws sticking frantically underneath the bathroom door trying to get in. A few times I forgot to lock the door and he managed to bang his way in like a gangster. In times like these, I felt like an actress in a B-grade cute horror movie. Oh did I mention he also meows incessantly and keeps watch outside the bathroom when he hears the shower running - like he is worried there's a tsunami? Quite a sweetheart, but jeez a gal needs some privacy.

One of his favorite pastimes is hopping onto my dining table and watching / sniffing intently while I eat. I can hear his telepathic thoughts like: "That sandwich smells so fine. Wanna share the love?" Every cupboard door or drawers that I use is the Most Urgent one he must inspect.

Sometimes when I'm rushing around, he trotters after me like he doesn't want to miss out the action. As a result I tripped a few times when six fast-moving feet got tangled.

But the worst faux pas is his perfectly timed deafening MEOWS when I'm in the middle of a work phone call. Sigh.

Me-time is now a distant memory for me. My dear comrade, you have been warned.

4) Humans vs Cats - Battle of Wits & Wills

Are cats really that smart? I can't say for sure but they're determined little fellas once they set their hearts. Theodore is quite mischievous and I honestly don't know if he'll ever grow out of it. Often he pretends to be half-asleep while planning his next move to dash into the forbidden bedroom or pounce on unsuspecting passersby.

Even if I tell him "NO" repeatedly, he will push things off the table, jump on top of the fridge, scratch the monitor etc. When it comes to his favorite dinner time, he is most persistent and will yeow my ears off. I've no problem feeding him, except he often demands dinner at 3pm. He understands "wait" and I often try to extend as many "waits" as possible till it's a reasonable time. In the meanwhile, he will return doggedly like The Terminator to check on his impending dinner. His doggedness will make him a great salesman or politician.

With cats it will always be a battle of their wits against yours. So I advise going with the flow and improvising along the way.

Chapter 4: Carrots & Sticks - Can Your Cat Be Trained?

They say cats don't respond to punishments like dogs. I think it's a yes and no.

Theodore doesn't show much remorse or memory of his misdeeds. But he does know when he has done something really naughty like pushing my cup off the table before running to hide under the couch. Even though he knows he is going to be in big trouble, he'll still do it again when he thinks I'm not looking or sometimes just in my face! With cats it's - sorry, not sorry.

Some cat deterrent methods are using a water spray bottle or flicking their ears. Sometimes I blow in his face if both my hands are occupied and especially when I'm cooking or washing. He finds it totally offensive and gives me a sourpuss face so I guess it works.

In some circumstances, I have to use "carrots" when "sticks" won't work. E.g. when he parked himself somewhere unreachable and refused to bulge. I'll lure him out with his favorite treats. Often I suspect he does it just to elicit more treats. Sigh.

Think out-smart rather than carrots and sticks - after all they are just a means to an end. Nowadays I no longer have the heart to water spray or flick his ears because I know he is just being a cat.

1) Does My Cat Recognize His Name?

Dog owners probably have a leg-up on this. Cats are more ambiguous and respond more to our tone and voice. They are known to respond better if trained as kittens. You can try rewarding a treat every time kitty responds to his name.

Theodore was estimated ten months old when I adopted him. I tried not to confuse him by calling him "baby", "kitty" or "sweetie pie". Every day I called him "Theodore" especially during mealtimes. Nowadays he definitely recognizes his name and will respond eight out of ten times even when he's out of sight. I knew for sure when one time he heard someone called "Theodore" on TV and immediately looked up.

Not only can you teach your cat to recognize his name, you can also teach simple commands like "sit" or "wait". Theodore also understands a few other words like: "wait", "sit", "down", "no", "clever boy", "bonito" etc. Cats are really highly intelligent animals that can be taught with some patience.

2) How To Litter Train My Cat?

Some kittens learn naturally from their mothers how to use a litter box. In the beginning, I was the cat mama as I'd carry and place Theodore in the litter box after his meals to remind him where the litter box is. Nowadays he will look for me and let out two short meows as his code word for - "Please cleanup my poop".

If you are starting from ground zero here are some tips:

- Start training with one room instead of free-run to localize accidents.

- Choose a large enough litter box for your cat to grow into adult cat size. Rule of thumb is one litter box to one cat.

- Litter box can be covered or uncovered. Some cats don't mind either. You might have to experiment if kitty refuses to use his hooded box.

- Place litter box in an accessible and quiet low-traffic area; just like how you'll prefer privacy in the toilet. Try another location if he refuses to use it.

- Do NOT place litter box near his sleeping, food and water area. Yes, they mind too.

- Choose the right litter and if he doesn't go for it, you might have to experiment.

- Use the correct recommended amount of litter which is normally two to four inches. It shouldn't be too much to create a mess, but enough for kitty to dig and bury.

- Clean litter box daily with fresh litter as cats are finicky about cleanliness. Regularly wash with warm water and mild detergent or some vinegar. For the first few weeks of training, leave some waste behind as a gentle reminder to kitty.

- Observe kitty's schedule and place him in the litter box after napping, playing or eating.

- Praise lavishly when he hops into his litter box and reward him with a treat when he does it correctly.

- If your cat has never used a litter box before, you will need to carry him and dig around some litter to show him how to cover his waste.

Don'ts:

- Do not scold or punish as it will just make him frightened. Pick him up and place him in the litter box instead so that he can make the connection.

- If he makes a mistake somewhere, scoop and place into his litter box to remind him.

- Clean accident spots thoroughly with an effective cleaner (or make your own bottle of natural all-purpose-cleaner with 1:1 water to distilled white vinegar), so that he won't return to the same crime scene. If it persists, try putting his food and water there to deter him.

- If the problem persists, you might want to consult the vet to rule out any medical problems such as urinary tract infections.

3) How To Play With My Cat?

Playing is a fun and great way to bond with your cat. It is important to play with your cat daily as it provides exercise for your cat (and yourself), prevents boredom which might lead to unwanted behavior e.g. chewing electrical cords or plastic bags. If you have a shy cat, it will also help to build confidence and trust. Playing also reduces stress for both cat and owner. Indoor cats who don't venture outside will also need playtime as stimulation, especially if they are still young and active.

Every cat is different so you have to find what floats kitty's boat. Here are some simple ones to start:

- Laser pointer. Be careful not to point it at your cat's eyes, TV or breakables. If you don't want to encourage jumping, point it towards the ground. I limit Mr. Laser with Theodore because I noticed he was getting frustrated at not being able to catch his elusive prey. Remember your cat needs the satisfaction of being able to catch their prey.

- Ping pong balls, tennis balls, crumpled papers, paper airplanes. Just toss and see your cat activate his hunting instinct. You can even try playing fetch. Your cat might bring the ball back to you or you can keep trying with some treats. You can store the toys with some catnip in a Ziploc first, to make them more enticing to kitty.

- Shopping bags are always enticing. Theodore loves checking out and jumping into any new shopping bag I bring home. The bigger the better for him. You can let him hide inside and use a feathery wand or toy to wriggle around the bag and watch him swap.

- Tablet and Smartphone games for cats are getting quite popular too. I downloaded a few fish and mouse games for Theodore but they didn't hold his interest for long.

- Toss your cat's kibbles across the room for him to chase and eat. Or you can use a treat ball puzzle. It will make him feel like he is hunting for his food.

Cats are really like imaginative little children. They can magically turn anything like bottle caps, straws, paperclips, twister tie, Q-tips, coins, toothbrushes into makeshift toys. Like children, you need to rotate their toys so that they don't get bored. Every day I'll put out a few toys for Theodore and keep the rest.

Theodore loves hide and seek kind of games. He will hide behind the door or box and bats at his favorite brown ribbon or some feathery wand especially if they come with some manmade sound effects. Yup, I'm one of those owners who sing silly made-up songs to her cat. He is very good at lunging and jumping in the air almost to my shoulders to catch Mr. Ribbon. When he needs timeout, he will bite Mr. Ribbon and pin it down with his body refusing to let go.

When in the mood, he will chase or pounce when I use the laser pointer or bounce some ping pong balls. When I roll the tennis ball towards him, he will just spread out like a goal post to receive it.

When it comes to playtime, I have to roll with Theodore's mood and timing which is usually late evenings. All in all, I think both of us have a pretty good daily workout.

4) Can Cats Walk On a Leash?

Bob the cat from the bestseller book and award winning movie "A Street Cat Named Bob" walks on a leash and even perch on his owner's shoulder like a giant parrot. His owner James trained him by getting him used to wearing a harness at home, and dragging it around before venturing outdoors.

Leash walking is handy if you want to bring kitty out on a trail walk or get some outdoor exercise. It is also a great way to bond together as kitty gets some fresh air, real trees and maybe some up-close small animals watching.

Steps:

- Introduce Mr. Harness by leaving it around for him to check it out.

- Let him try it on without fastening.

- Reward him with some treats as a positive association with Mr. Harness. Remove if he gets upset.

- Let him wear Mr. Harness during mealtime, so he won't get too distracted.

- When he is used to it, fasten the harness with one or two fingers space making sure it is snug so he won't escape.

- After a few days, attach the leash and let him walk around with the leash dragging behind.

- Practice around the house with the leash loose in your hands.

- Once kitty is ready, you can start slowly with your backyard or a small outdoor area where you can guard his escape.

- Go slow, go easy and make sure kitty is comfortable and enjoying it. Unlike dogs, some cats simply prefer napping to walking.

5) Responsible Use Of Cage

Is a cage or enclosure necessary for our beloved free spirited cats? Theodore has a free-run of the house except for a few restricted areas like closets and bathrooms. I never thought of using a cage even when he misbehaves. After all a cat is just being a cat. Some boo-boo's here and there does not warrant caging in my book just like we don't cage a child just because he is naughty.

It is cruel for cats to live their lives in a cage. But just like there are two sides to a coin, there are some exceptions when it is used responsibly:

- Pregnant or nursing female cats.

- To quarantine a sick cat from other pets till he gets better.

- To separate a cat that has not being tested for FIV and FeLV from healthy cats.

- To house an injured cat e.g. he is too hyper and his broken leg needs time to heal.

- To house feral cats in the process of being tamed.

- To use as litter box training for kittens. Use a cage big enough for mommy cat, kittens, litter box, food and water. The kittens will learn quickly by watching their mother use the litter box. Be sure to let mommy out to stretch her legs once in a while.

- Litter box training in a cage for adult cats with poor habits.

- Use a cage to introduce a new cat to your other cat or pets. The resident cat can check out his new roomie and get used to his scent. The new kitty will feel more secure in his cage. After a trial period when your resident cat is comfortable - no growling and puffing, the new roomie can be let out under supervision. Take a step backwards if things get rough.

- Temporary caging if you are having a big party and don't want to risk kitty getting spooked by strangers and going missing.

Please use a cage responsibly at all times.

Chapter 5: Cat Language & Personalities

1) Are You A Cat Person?

I have fond childhood memories of my Grandfather's two cats ignoring me while I spent hours watching them, intrigued. Other than providing them food and water, they seemed to require little else. Independent and low-maintenance - cats must be the way to go when I adopt. Besides, I didn't envy friends and neighbors who have to walk their beloved dogs daily, rain or shine.

Alas Theodore is only independent when he is bird-watching or in a food coma. Have you already guessed he is greedy by nature? Sometimes he will demand food or play depending on his mood and especially when I'm busy. Having a cat or any pet is never low-maintenance because they depend on you for everything.

The saving grace is cats sleep twelve to sixteen hours a day, which buys me some time to putter around without Inspector Theodore. Tip: Make good use of your window of time.

You might however have a totally zen and independent kitty that is different from mine. But you'll still need to set aside some time for playtime, clearing cat litter, feeding and general grooming. Well, a small price to pay for a contented kitty.

2) Your Cat's Personality & You

Are you curious about your cat's personality? Read on to find out which describes your cat.

The Alpha

This does not refer to a typical dominant leader of the pack animal, but rather how your cat interacts with you and his environment. Alpha cats are so confident that they want to manipulate their environment. They have a Napoleon complex, are highly intelligent, energetic and need to be kept busy and amused to stay out of trouble.

Theodore's fosterers have a typical Alpha cat - Genki is an athletic dark colored Tabby who literally bounces off from wall-to-wall. He is so smart he can open drawers and potato chips to share with his canine BFF, Patcher. His largest haul was destroying hundreds of dollars' worth of retail food items to the exasperation of his owners. He also habitually snitches his owners' food when they are not looking. For amusement he sometimes bullies the timid ones by biting out their fur. The last I heard Mr. Cane was keeping the mischievous cat in line.

If you have an alpha cat, you are up for the challenge of outwitting and keeping one step ahead of these crafty energetic felines. They'll even try to exert their dominance over you. Discipline might work for a while till they decide otherwise. You will probably get lots of laughter and tears from their antics. One thing for sure, it will never be a dull moment with these entertaining alpha cats.

The Beta

Beta cats are great talkers who are confident about getting us to change the environment. They will often remind you to refill their food, water or change their litter. They are sociable and like companionship. They are likely to get along with other cats. To get their cooperation, you need to communicate and negotiate with these little talkers. They love to follow you everywhere and watch what you are doing, especially if you are handling their property such as cat litter box, water or food. They are most likely to be doggy-cat personality and will come when called and sit on your lap. Beta cats make excellent door greeters to your visitors.

At home my self-appointed nosy little supervisor, aka Theodore, is definitely a Beta. He is extremely vocal and diligently "inspects" all incoming plastic bags, dirty gym clothes and visitors. He also inspects the cleaning of his cat litter box, water or food bowls. When I'm doing dishes, he will park himself right next to the sink to make sure I don't miss a spot. Like most cats, he is especially fascinated by running water faucets. But he doesn't like the wetness and will jump if some water accidentally splashes near him.

When in the mood, he becomes a door-greeter to any visitor or passerby. Once he charged towards the unsuspecting postman and scared the bejesus out of him. I lamely explained he was super excited because his favorite chicken treat was in the parcel.

Since Theodore fits a beta to a T, I learned to accept his chattiness and will even explain why he can't have his dinner at 3pm, 4pm, 4.05pm or 4.10pm. Yup, he bargains round the clock. Knowing his personality greatly improved our communication style and expectations. His constant vocal expression and deep-seated curiosity is just part of his personality makeup. Instead of expecting him to behave a certain way, I learn to work around it.

If you've got a beta cat, get ready for some serious feline conversations.

The Gamma

Gamma cats are quiet, gentle, shy, sweet and mellow. They don't know the environment can be changed. You need patience to win their trust and affection.

They are not fussy but need stability and routine to feel safe in their environment. They might have difficulty communicating, so you have to anticipate their needs and even check on their food, water or litter regularly. Otherwise they might suffer in silence. They can be stressed if in a large family with children and other pets.

They can be independent and are the best cats for not messing with our things. Be patient and fuss over them without being pushy, and they will prove to be devoted and cuddly companions.

I once encountered a lost Maine coon cat that hid in a corner looking extremely distressed. She did not make a single peep but stared pleadingly. Thankfully with some help we managed to trace her to a neighbor who didn't even realize she was missing. In retrospect, she was probably a Gamma cat, so quiet and unassuming that her owners didn't even realize her absence.

Alpha-Beta, Beta-Gamma, Beta-Alpha?

It is also possible for your cat to be a mix. I think Theodore is a beta-alpha as he doesn't mind being left alone and can play on his own.
Prior to adoption, Theodore did not display his vocal prowess and I had the false impression he was a quiet one as he seemed quite reserved. Well, as they often say - your cat chooses you. Nowadays I just see him affectionately as my expressive and attentive little inspector.

THEODORE'S PETTING CHART

3) How To Carry or Handle My Cat?

Theodore is my first cat, so it took some practicing and courage for both of us. Remember the rule of thumb is to let your cat come to you and don't rush. Offer your hand for your cat to sniff or head butt before gently petting his head or scratching his chin, as the safest region is his head. If your cat head bumps you, it means he wants some attention. If he has had enough, he will move away or give subtle signals. Don't overdo it, otherwise you might risk a bite or scratch.

Take note the belly is a no-go area. Do not be tempted even if they roll over invitingly with anime eyes. Exposing their belly means they feel relaxed and safe, it is not an invitation for a belly-rub like doggies. See but no touch.

I like to think Theodore will be less fussy if I've raised him as a kitten, but who knows? Every cat is different and you will know yours soon enough.

Steps:

- Go slowly and let your cat be familiar with you first. You might have to wait a few hours or days depending on your cat's temperament.

- Let your cat come to you by offering your hand for him to sniff or rub his chin.

- Don't make any sudden movements.

- If he bumps his head against you, it's a good sign he wants your attention.

- If he rolls onto his back and exposes his belly, it's a good sign as he trusts you.

- When you sense your cat is ready, pick him up by securing your hands firmly on his upper body and behind. Remember to hold firmly not tightly.

- Once your cat starts squirming or fidgeting, he has had enough and it is time to let him down.

- Let your cat know he can get down whenever he chooses to. This will create more trust for him to be carried by you.

- Rinse and repeat.

Warning: Cats over a few months old should not be picked up by the scruff of the neck as it will strain their spine and muscles tremendously.

I'll normally offer my hand for Theodore to sniff first so I don't startle him. Once I sense he is ready, I'll scoop him up with one hand supporting his underbelly and the other supporting his chest lightly. Initially he won't tolerate it and will get fidgety. So I started creating a positive association - each time I'll carry him to the shelf that contains his special treats. After a few positive reinforcements, he got used to being carried knowing he'll get a yummy reward. It worked wonderfully and he soon got used to being carried with his tail swishing in anticipation of a special treat. You can improvise a similar method with your cat's favorite treat or toy.

Depending on your cat, some like to be cradled on their backs like babies, carried over the shoulders or held on the lap. Experiment and find a style that suits both of you.

4) Tail-Speak: Body Language Of The Tail

Your cat's tail is a live telecast of his mood. Forget about the image of a happy dog's wagging tail; a cat's tail is totally opposite. When a cat's tail "wags" or rather whips, it means irritation, fear, aggression or simply stay-away.

When Theodore gets excited for his gourmet dinner, his tail will be erect and vibrating at the same time like he's chanting "Dinner, dinner, dinner..."

His most common tail expression is a question mark curved "?" It normally means he is bored and looking for some entertainment or adventure. "Hmm... what's interesting around here?"

When I come home, he often greets me with his tail held high in the air. This normally means confidence, contentment and friendliness. "Hiya!"

When he is enjoying being brushed, he shuts his eyes and does a low and slow side to side sweep with his tail. "Life's sooo good..."

During bird-watching, he will be totally absorbed with his tail lashing side to side. Sometimes he makes a strange chattering sound like he is talking to himself or he is trying to contain his frustrations.

Our neighbor's Husky named Sophie is a gorgeous redhead who is slightly younger but much bigger than Theodore. I often teased that his girlfriend was looking for him. Whenever she stops to greet Theodore at the gate, they will both act cool like a staring contest until one of them loses it and lets out a "Woof" or "Yeow". All hell breaks loose with gate banging and shoes flying. Theodore will transform into Incredible Hulk with his fur puffed up, back acutely arched and his puffy tail all stiff like an antenna, all the while hissing at Sophie to back-off his territory. My apologetic neighbor will quickly lead Sophie away, while I let The Incredible Hulk calm down and revert to his normal size as I clean Sophie's saliva off the gates. Sigh.

Tail tucked in-between his legs means he's frightened like when he is having his nails trimmed at the groomer and hissing at the same time reaching for a hand to bite. This is why I sometimes present his groomers with food because I'm so grateful to them.

After a while, you will be familiar with your cat's unique tail lingo which is often more telling than his poker face.

5) The Meows Or Yeows Language

Do you know cats do not meow at each other? Meowing is only reserved for us special humans. In fact, cats can make more than a hundred vocal sounds compared to dogs at only ten sounds.

At first Theodore's meowing seemed random. But as time goes by, I realized he is constantly expanding his repertoire of meows. I'm still learning his expanding cat language.

Here are some:

- Short sound - Theodore normally makes a short Yeow like "hi" when he greets or announces his grand entrance.

- Enthusiastic vocals with full capacity double triple meowing is Theodore's long-time-no-see greeting. He'll often use this if I've slept in later than usual, have been away the whole day or just hiding in the room.

- Sometimes he gives a distinctive two loud meows to request for toilet cleaning after doing No. 2.

- Chattering sound through the teeth means bird-alert or squirrels. He is expressing excitement and frustration that he can't reach the bird behind the window.

- Hissing means fight or flight and is very obvious. Theodore once hissed at a young neighbor who stared at him too long as cats think direct eye contact is a threat. Of course, Sophie the Husky received a fair bit of hissing too.

- Yowling or howling is my courtesy early morning wake-up call at 5am to feed him brekkie.

- Purring or vibrating sound normally means he is contented and welcomes a good head rub and chin scratch. Purring / vibrating is definitely my favorite sound and there are even scientific health benefits. Purr vibrations at 20-140 Hz is known to be therapeutic for many illnesses. This includes lowering stress, decreasing the risk of heart attacks, lowering blood pressure, heals infection, bones, muscles and injuries. I have heard of stories whereby cats will purr near their sick owners to help them heal. Maybe next time I could cure my headache with a Theodore on my head.

Chapter 6: Your Cat's Health

A healthy cat is a happy cat. The average lifespan of a domestic cat is fifteen years, so it's really important to take good care of our little furry companions.

1) Vaccination

Vaccinations and boosters are to help protect our cats against cat flu, feline leukemia (FeLV) and chlamydia. Your vet will advise you on the frequency. As Theodore is an indoor cat, his vet recommended a vaccine every two years from third year onwards. FeLV vaccine is also not necessary for an indoor cat, unless he is regularly exposed to other cats.

Note: Cat flu is an exclusive feline disease. The good news is you can't catch flu from your cat. Although the chances are low, if you have the flu or are feeling unwell, do distance yourself and take the usual precautions.

2) Annual Health Check

Even if your cat is still young or seems perfectly healthy, it's still highly recommended for an annual health examination to make sure everything is tip-top. You might also not realize your young two-year old cat is equivalent to twenty-four human years. Thereafter every additional cat year is equivalent to four human years.

1st year = 15 human years

2nd year = 24 human years

Every additional year = +4 human years

Examples:

a) Three-year old cat = twenty-eight human years

b) Five-year old cat = thirty-six human years

Take note of any health concerns or changes in your cat before the appointment. You can expect your vet to check - weight, eyes, ear mites, dental, heart rate, hair, skin and other abnormalities or blood tests if necessary. An annual checkup will also give your vet a chance to detect any early symptoms of disease, sometimes making a difference between life and death.

3) FIV / FeLV Test

This is an optional, simple, on-the-spot blood test done by the vet.

- FIV: Feline Immunodeficiency Virus; suppression of the immune system by attacking important cells of the cat's immune system. FIV is most commonly infected through bite wounds.

- FeLV: Feline Leukemia Virus can cause bone marrow suppression. FeLV is infected through saliva, grooming, sharing of bowls and casual contact with other cats.

I had this test done on Theodore as he was abandoned and living as a stray for a while before being rescued. Thankfully he tested negative. Infected cats might have a shorter life span but can live a relatively normal life. They have to be isolated from other cats to prevent further spreading. It's best to keep them indoors and provide a high quality diet, clean and stress-free environment. But otherwise, they can live happily just like normal cats.

You can minimize risks of both FIV/FeLV by:

- Keeping your cat indoors.

- Annual checkups and physical examinations at your vet to ensure kitty is in good health. Senior cats might require twice yearly examinations. Early diagnosis will help improve the quality of your cat's life with early treatment.

4) Should I Sterilize My Cat?

What Is Sterilization or Spaying?

- Sterilization means surgical removal of reproduction organs.

- Neutering is removal of testicles for males.

- Spaying is removal of ovaries and uterus for females.

- It can be done at 6 months of age or earlier if cat is in heat.

- Sterilization is considered a very low risk, 5-15 min surgery done under general anesthesia.

- Recovery time is 1-2 days.

- For males, no sutures are required. But you have to make sure the healing incision stays clean and dry.

- For females, there are a few sutures which will be removed 10 days post-op.

It is important to ear tip stray cats so that they won't be re-trapped for sterilization. But is it necessary for house pets? This mark could save your pet's life someday if he gets lost and is on his own in the world (some street cats were once house pets too). Their chances of being disposed or culled are minimized if they are identified as sterilized.

What Might Happen If You Don't Neuter Tom:

- Instead of being kinder to him, he will be at the mercy of hormones.

- He will suffer from wanderlust and try to escape even if he is an indoor cat.

- He will keep meowing at night and disturb your neighbors.

- He might contract FIV/feline AIDS if he gets into fights with other male competitors.

- He might get painful abscesses from cat fights.

- He will spray pungent urine all over your house e.g. walls, furniture.

- A male cat can potentially impregnate 1000 females in a year.

Good news is neutering eliminates the risk of testicular cancer and reduces the risk of prostate disease.

What Might Happen If You Don't Spay Molly:

- As above with Tom, she will endure fights and repeated mating.

- Studies show that the mating process is actually a rather painful experience for females. It is violent and stressful for them.

- Health issues if she gets pregnant too young.

- She will become very vocal when in heat, and attract every Tom cat to spray outside your house.

Good news is spaying before her first heat cycle will reduce or eliminate risk of mammary, ovarian and uterine cancer.

What Is Ear Tipping or Clipping?

Ear tipping is a small straight snip on the left ear - the universal mark for sterilized cats (for some countries it might be the right ear). It is a painless procedure done together with sterilization when the cat is under anesthesia. This is a helpful way to identify cats that have been fixed, so that they won't be neutered twice.

Is It The Right Thing To Do?

Do it for world peace... well, not exactly, but for overpopulation. Consider the plight of many stray and abandoned animals in our local shelters in need of good homes. Some are put to death because the shelters simply don't have the space or resources. Imagine, a breeding pair can produce 3-5 kittens at 3-4 times a year which means 9-20 kittens in a year! Well, just think about it.

My Personal Experience

My first visit with Theodore was postponed because he had just had his sterilization surgery. His wonderful rescuer RZ is an experienced community cat feeder who uses her own money bringing in strays for sterilization. RZ was also adamant about ear tipping and not leaving things to chance.

When we met, he was looking mighty fine and strutting around with a barely noticeable ear tip and missing *ahem*. One week later, after a mandatory house inspection and paperwork my beautiful boy finally arrived home-sweet-home.

P.S. I still keep in touch with Theodore's rescuer RZ occasionally sending her photos and videos to let her know he is well-loved. It was the goodness of her heart that led Theodore to us.

Note: You can check with your local animal shelters or rescue groups which often do sterilization for less. Theodore's sterilization and micro chipping was subsidized by the local government and cat welfare organization's stray cat sterilization program.

5) Fleas & Ticks Prevention

Fleas and ticks are both parasites that feed on animals' blood, causing flea allergy dermatitis or tick-borne illnesses.

A flea is a wingless insect that jumps, and thrives in warm climates. Once it finds a host (your cat) it will stay till it dies. It can live more than 100 days. A flea can lay 20-40 eggs daily and use the host to spread the eggs as he moves around.

Ticks are bigger and are an arachnid with eight legs. They prefer cooler climates and will move from host to host. It has a lifespan of a few weeks to three years. A tick can lay thousands of eggs at one time.

Fleas and ticks can bite humans too. In humans, flea bites result in small itchy red bumps. Tick bites usually have no symptoms, but can cause allergic reactions such as pain, swelling, rash or breathing difficulty.

Indoor cats can also get fleas from:

- Outdoor pets e.g. your neighbor's dog that often goes for walks in the park.

- Wild animals at the windows e.g. birds, squirrels or rodents.

- Our clothes if we've visited a park or wooded area.

- Our yards.

Symptoms include: Incessant scratching, open wounds, skin infection, fur loss.

Preventions:

- Keep your cat indoors

- Keep your home dry

- Avoid carpets as fleas love them

- If you own a yard, trim all tall grass, bushes, shrubs and remove all weeds.

Treatments:

- Visit your vet for oral medication.

- Flea tablets are known to work within 30mins but it only last a day (don't give those meant for dogs).

- Over counter shampoos, powders, combs.

- Clean and vacuum the entire house thoroughly.

- Use flea shampoo or flea sprays on all furniture, fabric and carpet.

- For minor infestations, shine a night light or table lamp over a shallow dish filled with dish detergent water and put it on the floor. This trap uses the light to attract the adult fleas and once they hop into it, the detergent will kill them.

- For serious infestation, consider DIY fogging or hire a professional exterminator.

The best cure is always prevention. Theodore's vet recommended the brand Revolution by Zoetis for prevention of fleas, heartworms, roundworms, hookworms and ear mites. It's also the only brand that is effective against ear mites. It can be easily applied by squeezing the contents of the tube onto the base of your cat's neck. Recommended once every two months for indoor cats or once monthly for outdoor cats.

6) Hairball Or Hair Raising Problem?

Hairball (trichobezoar) is caused by indigestible hair that is swallowed during grooming, and builds up in the stomach. If it doesn't pass through kitty's digestive tract via pooping, it will form a mass that has to be regurgitated.

What Does a Hairball Look Like?

I have heard horror stories of owners waking up in a stupor, only to be booby trapped by a slimy hairball while bare foot. Hairballs aren't rounded but more like wads of hair-undigested-food-goo. It most resembles wet cat poop, but I'm sure you can tell by the lack of smell.

You can minimize hairballs by:

- Frequent or daily brushing to reduce loose hair being ingested (especially longhaired cats). Preferably three to four times weekly for shorthair, and four to five minutes daily for longhaired cats.

  Besides using a regular pet brush, Theodore also likes a toothbrush to scratch his lower chin but sometimes it ends up in his mouth when he bites it. Regular brushing was a ritual I had to get him used to as he initially fought tooth and nail.
- Regular professional grooming.

- Distract kitty's excessive grooming with a new toy or better still playtime with you.

- Feeding hairball formula foods or treats.

- Add Omega-3 supplements to improve skin and fur, and aid in digestive system.

- Keep kitty regular by increasing high fiber food e.g. one to two teaspoon of cooked or canned pumpkin, one teaspoon of flaxseed, fish or olive oil, psyllium seed husk powder or a pinch of coconut fiber.

- Consider a grain-free low carbohydrate diet as it resembles our cats' original diet in the wild.

- Add good quality animal-sourced digestive enzymes to your cat's diet.

There is a popular remedy which involves putting a dab of Vaseline Jelly (yes the all purpose petroleum jelly) on the cat's paw. When the cat licks the petroleum jelly it will lubricate the digestive tract thus allowing the hairs to pass out. This method is debatable, as some claim petroleum jelly, which is actually crude oil, use in our cars and lawn mowers is toxic and cancer causing. Our cat is not a car, so why risk it? Consider safer all-natural alternatives made with slippery elm, papaya or coconut oil.

Symptoms:

Hairballs that don't pass can cause excessive vomiting, bloated stomachs, loss of appetite, lethargy, constipation or diarrhea. An internal blockage can become life threatening and need surgical removal. It can also be a sign of inflammatory bowel disease. If you notice any symptoms, please see a vet soon.

Alternatives:

Kitty coughing out one to two hairballs a year is considered normal. But in truth, our cats' digestive tract should be able to handle this hairy problem. They call this the bane of modern domesticated cats. Or is it?

One theory is that cats in the wild do not eat high fiber foods or lubricants. As true carnivores, cats in the wild eat pure carnivorous diets of rodents, an average of nine mice a day. In contrast, modern cat food contains lots of carbohydrates and fiber which might cause impaired gut and vomiting.

The alternative? Consider a grain-free and low carbohydrate diet that resembles our cats' natural diet. There have been favorable reports of owners reporting a reduction in hairball vomiting as well as slimmer and healthier cats.

Theodore had only presented me with a hairball one year after he came. It resembled brown vomit with some unidentifiable wad of object. It was found in the morning so I did not see him in action (not that I want to).

Besides his grain-free diet, it is probably because he is not fastidious about personal grooming. In fact he is so lax with his own grooming that I often use a wet tissue to clean his face. Maybe he thinks I'm his part-time mummy cat?

7) Foods You Should NOT Feed Your Cat

- Onions, garlic and chives can cause gastrointestinal upset.

- Tuna that is canned contains levels of mercury, salt and oil in it.

- Milk or other dairy products can cause diarrhea and stomach upset.

- Alcohol: beer, liquor or wine are all damaging on our cat's liver. Just two teaspoons of whisky can cause coma, another one tablespoon can kill it.

- Grapes and raisins can cause kidney failure and vomiting.

- Caffeine: coffee, tea, cola, Red Bull, cocoa, chocolate, some cold medicines and painkillers. Side effects include rapid breathing, heart palpitations, muscle tremors and fits. Take note chocolate is especially lethal for cats and dogs.

- Candy and gum: Especially those with xylitol; it can lead to liver failure.

- Fat trimming and bones. The fats can cause intestinal upset and bones can cause choking.

- Raw Meat, fish or eggs: Risks of salmonella, E. coli, skin allergies, convulsion or coma.

- Dog food diet will cause malnutrition in cats.

- Overdose of liver can cause vitamin A toxicity which leads to deformed bones or death.

- Raw yeast dough if ingested will swell inside your cat's stomach leading to severe pain and poisoning.

- Avocado contains persin which is found on its pit, skin, bark and leaves. It can cause respiratory problems, heart failure or edema.

- Over the counter human medicine. Please give only what your vet recommends and keep your medicine out of reach.

8) What Foods Can I Share With My Cat?

Well, if you are so inclined to share your food with your cat you can share your pizza, cheeseburgers, doughnuts... Just kidding!

Vegetables e.g. baked carrots, cooked pumpkin, broccoli, winter squash or chopped greens. Make sure to wash thoroughly and avoid indigestible foods such as raw carrots.

Fish e.g. tuna. Take note of mercury contents in fish like tuna, salmon and swordfish.

Cooked eggs e.g. hard-boiled or scrambled eggs. Never give raw eggs and risk salmonella and E. coli. Also watch out for any egg allergies.

Meat - Cooked poultry like steamed chicken breast is the best option.

If kitty is already eating a good quality diet, do practice in moderation.

9) Plants That Are Toxic & Fatal To Cats

"Roses are red, violets are blue, but not all are safe for kitty."

Do you know some plants are toxic to our kitties? Symptoms include difficulty in breathing, drooling, swallowing, vomiting, diarrhea, excess drinking and urinating or irregular heart beat. Severe cases can lead to acute kidney failure resulting in death.

List of plants toxic to cats:

- Amaryllis

- Autumn Crocus

- Azaleas and Rhododendrons Caladium

- Castor Bean

- Chrysanthemum

- Creeping Charlies

- Cyclamen

- Dieffenbachia

- English Ivy

- Kalanchoe

- Lilies (all types)

- Marijuana

- Mistletoe

- Oleander

- Philodendron

- Poinsettia

- Pothos

- Sago Palm

- Spanish thyme

- Tulip and Narcissus bulbs

- Yew

If in doubt, it is best to remove the plant as some kitties have the tendency to chew on plants (unless it is cat grass).

10) Essential Oils That Are Toxic To Cats

Established research has found that certain essential oils are toxic to our cats and can cause serious liver damage, liver failure, seizures and even death. This is because their liver does not have specific enzymes that can properly process compounds found in essential oils.

List of essential oils toxic to cats:

- Basil

- Cinnamon

- Citrus

- Clove

- Eucalyptus

- Laurus Nobilis

- Melaleuca Quinquenervia

- Mountain Savory

- Oregano

- Pennyroyal

- Peppermint

- Pine

- Sweet Birch

- Tea Tree

- Thyme

- Wintergreen

- Ylang Ylang

Do note that the above list is not exhaustive and each cat reacts differently. For example, lavender essential oil is considered generally safe for cats but it doesn't mean that your own cat is okay with it. Never apply directly onto their skin, feed your cat essential oils or leave them trapped in a room with an essential oil diffuser. Always use essential oils with caution, and if in doubt avoid using them around your cat.

Symptoms of poisoning:

- Coughing

- Difficulty breathing

- Lethargy

- Loss of appetite

- Low body temperature

- Low heart rate

- Panting

- Pawing at mouth or face

- Redness or burns on lips, gums or skin

- Salivating

- Tremors

- Uncoordinated gait

- Vomiting

- Watery nose or eyes

- Wheezing

11) How To Handle Asthma & Allergies

Most people think it is pet's fur, but it is actually the dander i.e. flecks of skin shed and saliva we are reacting to. These particles are too microscopic to be seen by naked eyes.

Prevention:

- Designate a restricted bedroom for retreat in case of asthma or allergic reaction. My housemate has asthma so her bedroom was off-limits in the beginning. He did trigger her in the first few weeks, but she eventually got over it and is now asthma free around him. We don't know how, but somehow Theodore made her lungs stronger than before. Anyway, she could never say no to him kneading biscuits on her comforter.

- Minimized carpets, rugs, mats, soft toys and other similar items. I replaced my door mats with rubber ones and the house has been reduced to one couch throw.

- Invest in a HEPA (high-efficiency particulate air) filter. A true HEPA can trap 99.97% of dust particles that are 0.3 microns e.g. pet dander, tobacco smoke, dust mites, pollen and mold spore.

I find my HEPA filter very effective and also great at removing odor from the house. The HEPA filter only traps pet dander that is floating in the air, so the next step is to vacuum those trapped in e.g. carpets and rugs.

- Vacuum regularly. I find myself vacuuming way too often since Theodore's arrival. My vacuum also comes with a HEPA filter and I'm always amazed at the amount of fur it sucks up. Things I regularly vacuum include couches, scratch post, beds, office chairs and even the window mesh.

- Wash bed sheets, comforters, covers regularly and in hot water for best results.

- Wash hands often to avoid transfer of dander to face or eyes.

- Feed kitty a balanced diet = healthier skin = less dander and shedding.

- Put someone else in-charge of litter box.

- Allergy shots as last resort.

If someone at home has asthma, allergies or illness, please have a serious discussion before committing to a pet. Usually people don't abandon their children just because they are "inconvenient". Likewise a pet is also part of the family. Make sure it's a unanimous decision before committing to a pet.

12) Does My Cat Need A Bath Or Grooming?

Generally cats do not smell because they don't sweat like dogs, but they sweat through their paws. I send Theodore regularly to the groomers as he does have a habit of getting into dusty cupboards or hidey holes I never knew existed (and therefore never clean).

The main reason though is the trimming of his nails. Since I didn't have Theodore as a kitten, he was not introduced to nail clipping at an early age. At the groomers, it sometimes takes three people to do the job i.e. two to hold him and one brave soul to clip as he is extremely finicky about his hind legs. If you have a kitten, start introducing Mr. Clipper as soon as possible.

Regularly trimmed nails also mean less damage to your skin and furniture. Theodore can get over-zealous during playtimes and scratched me accidentally. It stings like a paper-cut, so keep some antiseptic cream nearby. I use an organic cream that is good for both pets and humans.

My vet who has three outdoor cats does not think bathing is necessary, unless they fell into some mud. It's really up to your personal preference... you could even try a DIY spa for kitty at home.

13) Accidental Bites And Scratches

A common bewildering problem cat owners face is our cats' Dr. Jekyll and Mr. Hyde personality. Does this sound familiar? Your cat purred contently as you petted and gave a good chin scratch here and there. Kitty seemed so pleased with your performance and then without warning whirled around and "rewarded" you with a bite. Ouch!

WTH happened? Normally I'll dish the silent treatment to let him know that was bad behavior. Even though I follow the cat body rules and refrain from petting his sensitive areas, he still misbehaves sometimes. It rarely happens nowadays as I've also gotten better and quicker at reading his body language.

Often cats have no pause button between "pleasure" and "annoying". But with some practice, you can read your cat's body language. E.g. Kitty starts swatting, moving away or his tail is swishing in an irritated rhythm. The easiest solution is to read the signals before things get out of hand.

Another common thing is play aggression. E.g. Theodore hides under the table and crouches with his ears flattened, pupils dilated and tail swishing in anticipation of pouncing at his prey, aka me. By now I'm familiar with all his usual booby traps, and will just announce "I see you!" to foil his surprise attack.

Sometimes accidents do happen. E.g. Theodore gets excited during playtime and scratched me. Or he pounced on me from behind and accidentally scratched my leg. To counteract, I will walk away and pretend like I'm in "great pain". After a while he got it, and is now much gentler when playing. Even his pouncing is reduced to just a tap on my legs or behind. I really think our cats are intelligent enough to know they hurt us and learn to play "nice".

I don't share with non-cat folks about cat bites or scratches because I think it send a wrong message. But to someone considering having a cat for the first time, I've to be honest that some biting and scratching will happen. But they will cease with some patience and training.

Please remember our cats' claws and teeth are meant for defending and hunting. By nature cats lay in wait, stalk and pounce. Since our cats are domesticated, we are often their only "entertainment".

Initially I didn't realize Theodore's pouncing was his cue for playtime. Now we make playtime a regular thing, and I try my best to accommodate his playtime requests.

Try to discourage rough play, biting and scratching. Start correcting poor behavior before it becomes a bad habit. But refrain from disciplining and shouting at your cat. It will only confuse or frighten him. Instead, timeout and withdraw your affection. Your cat will soon get the message this is not fun anymore and learn to adhere.

It's important to commit to regular playtime to wear out your cat. Occupy your cat with toys that he can sink his teeth into (instead of you), and a good scratch post for him to sink his claws into as well.
If you do get bitten or scratched, please wash under running water and put on some antiseptic cream. Cats' bites and scratches might sting a bit. Sometimes Theodore's bite even leaves some light bruising around it.

Tip: It will help a lot to trim kitty's nails regularly.

14) Rescue Remedy For Pets (The original Bach Flower remedies)

I really need to mention this amazing natural stress relief for pets. Initially I had a lot of problems with Theodore as he was very highly strung. But once I started putting 4 drops into his food, he started to calm down. Even till today, I'll put a few drops into his food before going to the groomers or vet. On certain days when he is acting restless and highly strung, I also give him a few drops to calm him down. I can't explain why it works, but it really did work wonders for Theodore. If you're having some problems with your cat, you can try this remedy safely.

Rescue Remedy helps animals with:

- Fear

- Stress

- Anxiety

- Loneliness

- Depression

- Jealousy

Note: Get the Rescue Remedy for Pets that is alcohol-free. I normally order my supply online.

Chapter 7: Feline Fetish & Bizarre Behaviors

Since Theodore is my first cat, some of his behavior was totally baffling to me initially.

1) Why Does My Cat Sleep Zzzzzz So Much?

It is really genetic that our cats sleep an average of 15 to 20 hours a day with kittens and older cats sleeping more. Cats are crepuscular animals which means they are most active between dusk and dawn. This explains why Theodore often wakes me up around 5am for kibbles, as it was his natural reaction to the sun rising.

During the day, they will catnap in-between meals. Catnap means light sleep. Well, you know the one where our cat is just sleeping with one-eye-open and ready to spring to action in a millisecond?

During rainy or cold days, they sleep and yawn more just like us. They also dream and twitch or move their whiskers and eyelids. Some short-nosed breeds e.g. Persian and Himalayan even snore.

Essentially all this beauty sleep is our kitty's way of conserving energy and repairing their bodies and 75% of it is catnap.

Theodore's late-night favorite pastime is hiding in shadows and pouncing on unsuspecting prey aka human. He is so sneaky that his collar bell doesn't even make a tinkle. In the middle of the night when everyone is asleep, I can hear him chasing ping pong balls and ramming into his cat tunnel. I always like this independent part of him that he can entertain himself.

2) Why Does He Keep Showing Me His Rear End?

Theodore's favorite position when I'm petting him at knee level is he will move his body forward and position his behind strategically in my face. At first I thought he was being rude, signaling he had enough petting or wanted behind petting.

Apparently your cat showing his behind is the equivalent of hugging your BFF. Showing his vulnerable behind means he is showing trust and affection for you. Some recommend correcting by gently repositioning, but I prefer to let him be a cat and enjoy his BFF hugs.

3) Why Is He Brushing or Rubbing Against Me?

Theodore tends to brush against me especially when my hands are full with dishes at the kitchen sink and powerless to his advances.
The short answer is your cat is showing his affectionate greeting. The long and sinister answer is your cat is marking you with his scent and staking his claim. Congrats, you are now part of His Highness' property.

4) Head Bumps

Same as above - marking you with his scent. Cats prefer to be touched on their heads; so it could also be his way of encouraging you to stroke or scratch his head. Theodore will close his eyes when enjoying a good scratch around his head, chin and ears. Pretty much like when we enjoy a good massage.

5) Eye Contact: Staring & Slow Blink

Contrary to humans, our cats view staring or direct eye contact as an intimidation or threat. The dominant cat will often stare down the other cat until he flees.

I find this to be true as there were a few times Theodore caught me admiring his sweet potato eyes and retaliated by jumping to my shoulder level.

Tip: When approaching an unfamiliar cat, make yourself unthreatening by avoiding direct eye contact.

Slow blink is the preferred way to make eye contact with your cat. Try slow blinking (think sleepy eyes) or winking to communicate with your cat. If your cat gives you a slow blink or flutter - it is a sign of trust and love. Theodore sometimes squint at me when he is on the brink of falling asleep; meaning he is relaxed and trusting enough to nap in my presence.

6) What Your Cat Licking You Means

If your cat licks you, it is his way of "petting" and bonding with you. Of course he is also marking you as his property. Cat's tongues feel like sandpaper, so it takes some getting used to. If it is your feet, it's because cats like salt. Usually after a run, my feet are like an irresistible salty popsicle to Theodore which is my cue to dash to the shower.

7) "Love Bites"

Nibbling or "love bites" is considered an upgrade from licking. Sometimes when I'm petting or scratching Theodore's chin, he will give me a sudden nip. My startled response is always a "Yelp" followed by a gentle tap on his head. Love bite or not, it hurts.

Cats can be over stimulated from too much petting, especially the base of the tail. Watch out for a sudden swat or bite which means time-out.

8) Why Is My Cat Kneading Biscuits?

One of Theodore's morning rituals is to hop onto my bed, the moment I open the bedroom door. He will start purring and kneading on the crumpled blanket like in a trance. He does this kneading by alternating his front paws to knead rhythmically. He looks so blissful and content that I don't have the heart to interrupt my little baker's rhythmic kneading. "So what bread are you making for mama today?"

One common theory on kneading is they are imitating their kitten-hood of kneading to stimulate milk from mummy. Adult cats find this nursing motion comforting. Some will paw, purr and drool as well.
If he does kneading on your lap - he is showing his affection and saying he loves you and also marking you as his property. I have not experienced this personally as Theodore is not a lap cat. But I heard it can be uncomfortable because of their nails digging in. Gently let your cat down if it gets too intense. After all love hurts sometimes.

9) Why Is My Cat Bringing "Gifts"?

Cats are notorious for bringing "gifts" to their beloved human. These "gifts" are not your typical flowers and candies, but small dead or half-dead creatures like rodents, lizards, bugs, grasshoppers etc. Consider this a huge compliment as your cat is showing you his deep affection and sharing his hunt with his beloved family member (who is also an inferior hunter).

What to do?

Put on your best Oscar award acting and promptly rearrange your horrified face (cats understand our body language). Refrain from screaming or yelling at the gift, or him or both. The right etiquette is to thank him for the gift and dispose of it discreetly when he is not looking.

Tip: How do you react when you receive an unwanted gift? "Errr thank you, it's nice of you." Got it?

I haven't had such a privilege since Theodore is an indoor cat. The closest "gift" he left was some torn out grass carpet at my bedroom door, which in my morning blurriness thought was a dead grasshopper - Phew.

10) Incurable Seat Snatchers

Cats are incurable seat snatchers - be it your favorite chair, couch or bed. Chances are you'll find sneaky kitty snuggly in your favorite seat the moment you get up to get a drink or answer a phone call. Theodore's favorite is an ergonomic office chair he likes to nap on. He likes it especially after I have "warmed" it. He will politely meow for me to get up before hopping on (no sharing for this feline). Theodore's fosterers advised me not to give up my "throne" as he is asserting his dominance. But I caved and rather than resisting his meowing, poking and prying, I now use a standby plastic stool. Well at least now I can work in peace while he snoozes.

Why your cat snatched your seat:

- Kitty really likes your good taste in chair

- Kitty likes your familiar scent on the chair - so much that he wants to put his own scent and fur all over it

- Cats prefer warmed seats just like most people prefer cold beers

- The grass is always greener on the other side was really referring to cats not cows.

11) Molesting Your Computer

The computer and keyboard being warm is a natural magnet to most cats. Theodore will slump across the keyboard and mouse especially when I'm in the middle of an important email. I now make it a habit to save my work periodically. He will pretend to close his eyes and Zzzz on my desk while holding my keyboard hostage.

My tactics: 1) Remove him physically at my own peril of waking a sleeping cat 2) Lure him out with treats or toys 3) Take a toilet break 4) Change to wireless keyboard and mouse or laptop.

12) Why Does My Cat Chew Plastic Bags?

One morning I had a fright when I thought Theodore missed his litter box and defecated on the kitchen floor. After braving myself for a closer inspection, I realized it was a pile of purple color bile? Hairballs? Nope. Did he have eggplants? Nope. That's when it hit me. He was chewing compulsively on a flimsy purple plastic bag I had brought home last evening. Thankfully he was alright for the rest of the day. Now, all plastic bags are safely hidden away.

So Why Are They Attracted To Plastic Bags?

- Food store plastic bags carry lingering food scent which makes them attractive.

- Some plastic bags are coated with cornstarch, stearates or gelatin making them attractive.

- Some cats enjoy the crinkly noises of plastic bags.

- Possible dental issues - please check with your vet.

- Chewing plastic can be a sign of anxiety problems like nail biting in humans.

Plastic bags are hazardous to cats. If your cat is drawn to them, please keep them in a safe place and use covered bins with lids.

13) Why Does My Cat Chew Electrical Cords?

Chewing on live wire is very dangerous and can cause burned tongue, missing teeth, electric shock, choking and even death.

- Boredom is usually the top reason, especially with young cats. Distract him with chew toys to satisfy his gnawing. Or get some cat grass e.g. oats or wheat for him to chew. Up your daily playtime to tire him out. Young cats will normally outgrow this habit.

- Possible dental or health issues. Please visit the vet as it can be a sign of insufficient dietary needs.

Preventions:

- Wrap or hide cords with rubber covers, PVC tubes, cable management box, aluminum foil, double-sided tape or bubble wrap.

- Tape or Velcro all dangling cords down to make them less appealing to kitty.

- Use pet deterrent spray to coat wiring or DIY your own hot sauce, lavender oil or citrus oil but avoid salt as cats love it.

- Switch to wireless technology e.g. cordless headphones, speakers.

- Hide small appliances like phone charges in drawers when not in use.

- Rearrange furniture to block or hide cables. E.g. Push the TV console against the wall leaving no gap for kitty to squeeze through.

Although Theodore doesn't have a penchant for cords, I use PVC tubes and cable management boxes to hide my nest of computer wires. Now everything looks much neater and safe for him to nap on my desk.

14) Why Is My Cat Running Bonkers After Pooping?

Sometimes after doing his No. 2 Theodore will bolt like a rocket from his litter box at one end of the house to the other. I often joked it was so smelly that he literally rocketed away.

Here are a few theories:

- They run because in the wild the smell of poop will attract predators.

- It can be a sign of digestive problems, discomfort from food allergies or infection, UTI (urinary tract infection), kidney stones.

- Some cats get "poo-phoria" (pleasurable sensation with defecating), and they run like crazy to burn off the "high".

- They can't stand the smell (my favorite theory).

- Our cats are flaunting their accomplishment and calling for attention (cleanup crew please).

My observation is Theodore was high on "poo-phoria". He actually seems elated and super energetic after doing No. 2. Sometimes he does this bolting after No. 1 too.
If your kitty grimaces in discomfort or you suspect it is medical, please visit the vet immediately.
Meanwhile this remains another mystery about our enigmatic felines.

15) Does Your Cat Cover His Poop?

In the wild cats bury their waste to throw predators off their scent. If your cat does this, he is acknowledging you as the "dominant cat" in the household.

My experience with Theodore is inconsistent - sometimes he does and sometimes nope. Maybe he can't make up his mind who is the alpha? Or modern cats no longer feel threatened?

From a cleaning perspective, I prefer him not to hide his disposals. Imagine Easter egg hunt with a different kind of egg. So much easier if it's just out in the open waiting to be bagged.

Note: Normal poop frequency is once to twice daily or alternate days. If it has been more than two days - try adding some fiber like cooked pumpkin; if it persists please see a vet.

16) Is That My Cat Or A Baby Crying?

A friend commented Theodore's loud "mrrrrr-meoooww" sounded uncannily like her baby's cries. It turned out she was right. These urgent solicitation purrs at 220-520 Hz has similar frequency range to babies' cries at 300-600 Hz. Wow, I'm officially impressed our cats use science to solicit food.

"Baby cries" are our cat's acoustic ruse to demand food. It is supposed to both irritate and appeal to owner's nurturing instincts toward a hungry baby. For me it's 99% irritation, so I guess I've little maternal instinct.

17) Pouncing Tigger

Does kitty pounce on you like a Tigger? Sometimes Theodore will hop and pounce on my legs or behind when he wants to play. Initially I didn't know what he wanted and even got a few scratches from his over enthusiasm. Once I figured he wanted to play, I'll get out his favorite Mr. Ribbon or some feathery wand. After a few rounds of chasing and jumping, he will be relaxed and contented after letting out all his excess energy. Theodore is relatively independent but I noticed he gets restless if he doesn't expend his excess energy. Ideally spend ten to fifteen minutes a day playing with your cat, especially if they're cooped up indoors or you're away the whole day. This also helps greatly to bond with your cat.

18) Cat Loaf aka Turkey, Chicken Pose or Hovercat

This is the famous pose cat owners like to post on the internet of their cats. Your cat is actually tucking his paws and tail under his body to keep warm. Our cat's body temperature is lower than ours at 100-102.5°F. This explains why they are drawn to computers, heaters or warm seats.

19) The Truth About Catnip

Catnip is a fragrant herb from the mint family which some kitties can't get enough of. There are no harmful side effects. When smelled it causes a short euphoric bliss or drooling in our kitties. If eaten, it acts as a sedative but an overdose can cause vomiting and diarrhea.

Theodore normally turns dreamy and mellow after sniffing and hugging his catnip rainbow toy. But some cats might turn into aggressive playfulness and start attacking things. Catnip triggers different types of reactions in different cats. But not all cats are addicted or drawn to catnip, Theodore can do without his catnip for weeks.

You can store the catnip toy or leaves in a Ziploc to retain freshness and for ration. The recommended use is once every few days and around ten to fifteen minutes. You can also rub some dried catnip leaves on kitty's scratch post or new toys to encourage him to use it. The catnip leaves can be stored in the fridge to retain freshness. Be careful not to get catnip onto your beloved couch or carpet.

Note: Not all catnips are genuine. I buy the brand "Yeowww!" for Theodore as it is 100% organic catnip and made in USA. It was highly recommended by Theodore's fosterers as the only catnip that works for their numerous cats.

Chapter 8: Fun Facts & Myths

1) Do Cats Have Nine Lives?

It's a popular myth which probably came about because of cats' amazing ability and agility to always land on their feet.

Others:

- In ancient Egypt, cats were worshipped and deemed sacred and revered creatures with supernatural powers. Based on ancient Egyptian numerology anything 3 x 3 was of great importance and thus they honor cats with 3 x 3 lives: 9.

- Atum-Ra the Egyptian sun god known as the Ennead or the Nine often took the form of a cat to visit the underworld.

- There's an old English proverb describing the nature of cats; "A cat has nine lives. For three he plays, for three he strays, and for the last three he stays".

Some of my guests innocently asked why I meshed up my windows as they assumed my "nine lives" cat will survive a 6-storey fall. I (internal eye-roll) explained to them this is a myth, and a cat or any living thing will definitely be critically injured or die from such falls. You will be surprised it is not children but adults who are misinformed as well. Sometimes common sense is not that common. So let's educate; our kitties only have one precious life like everybody else.

P.S. I have witnessed Theodore missing and falling off table tops before. It was totally unglamorous and proved cats do not always land on their feet.

2) Why Do Some Cats Have Pink Noses & Pink Paw Pads?

I was intrigued why some cats have pink noses and paw pads, while Theodore has liver color nose and black pads.

The color of our cat's nose and paw pads is related to their fur color. Well, just like if you have brown hair then brown eyebrows. Therefore black cats have black noses, white cats have pink noses, gray cats have gray noses, orange cats have orange noses etc. Multicolor cats, known as Calico, can have multicolor paw pads e.g. three black and one white.

3) Cats Have Unique Nose Print

Do you know our cat's nose is as unique as our fingerprints? No two kitty's noses are alike. Cat passport with unique nose print?

Our cat's nose is his most important sense organ and has 200 million scent receptors. Kitty's sense of smell is fourteen times stronger than ours. Which is why our cats are very fussy about the cleanliness of their litter box. Just imagine if everything you smell is magnified fourteen times, slightly funky will become super duper smelly.

When our cats lick their noses, it is because they are resetting it by removing any residue smell. It is also smell not flavor that stimulates their appetite. Which is why every time I open a can of tuna, Theodore will appear at lightning speed.

4) Paw Pads aka Beans, Beanies or Jelly Beans

Our kitty's paw pads are also known affectionately as: beans, beanies or jelly beans.

- Cats are digitigrades walkers which means they walk tiptoe. This is how Theodore can routinely spook me; even though he wears a collar with a bell he can approach without a tinkle.

- Cats' paw pads are very sensitive to hot and cold; which is probably why Theodore is smart enough to stay away from the burning stove and hot kettle.

- There are glands tucked between their paw pads which allow them to scent when they scratch their post or your favorite couch.

- Our kitties sweat through their paws, which is why sometimes I see Theodore's paw prints on my kitchen countertop or floor.

Have you tried feeling your kitty's soft paw pads? It's definitely one of my favorite parts of anatomy. Amazingly soft and cushy. Sometimes Theodore looks suspiciously at me when I hold on a tad too long for his liking.

5) The Long & Short About Whiskers

Rule No. 1 - Thou shalt not groom, trim or cut kitty's whiskers. No-no! Cats' whiskers are unlike our hair. They are known as vibrissae or tactile hairs with sensitive touch receptors like our fingertips. We don't cut our fingertips and likewise with our cats' whiskers.

Our cats' whiskers are a sensory organ with a rich supply of nerves and blood vessels. It enables them to gauge tight spaces, detect vibrations or visually measure distances which enable them to do all their acrobatics feats. Messing with their whiskers will make them disoriented and scared as they can't gauge their environment.

Cats' whiskers appear on their muzzle, cheeks, above eyelids, ears, jaw and wrists or forelegs. Our kitty's whiskers are also mood tellers. If kitty is threatened or upset, you will see taut pulled back whiskers or pointing forward when hunting his favorite toy.

Our kitty's whiskers do shed and grow back like hairs. I've heard of owners whose hobby is collecting their cat's whiskers. I've found a few of Theodore's whiskers and have no desire to collect them, but they make good makeshift toothpicks - just kidding.

6) Do Cats Fart?

Absolutely. I had the privilege of being gassed a few times by Theodore's silent bomb. Cats fart for the same reasons humans fart. Their high-protein diet with large amount of sulfur could also produce some lethal stinky gas.

There's a debate if cats' fart have sound. So far Theodore's farts have been silent, so I had no audible warning to clue me in. As the saying goes - "If a tree falls in a forest and no one is around to hear it, does it make a sound?"

As you probably already guessed, our feline friends feel no shame or embarrassment whatsoever.

"To fart is human, to fart & act nonchalant is cats" - Meow Tze

Note: If your cat has excessive gassing with signs of bloated tummy, vomiting, diarrhea or loss of appetite, please see the vet.

7) Do Cats Sweat Or Pant?

On a hot day we humans sweat a lot and will probably pant like dogs too if it helps. But Theodore with all that fur seems as cool as a cucumber; just grooming and minding his own business. Even with heavy duty deodorant I don't smell half as nice as him. Why?

Our cats do sweat, but through their paws which have sweat glands thus resulting in wet paw prints you probably see around the house. To cool themselves, they will sprawl out under shady spots. By grooming, they use their saliva to lower their body temperature.

However, extreme heat can cause cats to pant and heat stroke is lethal as it can cause organ failure. To cool down kitty, adjourn into some air conditioning, wipe him down with a wet towel and offer some cool water.

Note: Never leave your kitty in the car even if it's just for a few minutes or with a cracked window as the temperature can reach 110°F in just 30 minutes, and 70°F is warm enough to cause heat stroke.

8) Do Cats Have Fur Or Hair?

Our cats actually have both, as their whiskers are also known as tactile hairs. Both fur and hair are made of keratin. The difference is human hair tends to grow much longer, while most fur stops growing at a set length. Therefore hair or fur can be used interchangeably on our fur balls or hairballs.

9) Why Do Cats Shed Fur?

Cats shed fur to remove dead fur from their bodies. Indoor cats shed all year round while outdoor cats shed during spring and fall. Only healthy cats shed fur, so consider it a good sign.

With Theodore, shedding is a daily affair with tufts of fur rolling around and constant vacuuming. You can minimize shedding with frequent brushing or you can try using a normal lint roller which I found quite effective and acceptable to my cat. Otherwise you can just let nature takes its course.

Note: If your cat is losing excessive clumps of fur or his skin has bald patches and looks irritated, please see your vet.

10) Can Cats Taste Sweet?

Cats can't taste sweet because their taste buds lack sweet receptors. Some cats fancy fruit, cake or ice cream but probably more for the smell, texture or other flavors. Meat is their all-time favorite.

11) Can Cats See Color?

Our feline friends can see colors but less vibrant than humans, like low resolution vs high definition. They can discern between red, blue and yellow. They are most sensitive to blue-violet and greenish-yellow ranges. When shopping for kitty's next toy, pick his favorite blue or yellow.

12) Why Do Cats' Eyes Get Big / Dilate?

Have you ever seen that startled look on your cat's face? Sometimes I catch Theodore red-handed doing something really illegal and he will look at me with anime eyes.
Our cats don't just dilate their eyes at night or in low light to see better. Their eyes also communicate emotion and can dilate any time due to surprise, interest, fear, anxiety, defensiveness or excitement.

13) Do Cats Watch TV?

Theodore watched the entire "Nine Lives" movie by sitting on top of the TV console and blocking half the TV, with his nose inches away from the screen. Unless the actors are his own species, he is not interested in TV shows. Some cats do take to TV especially if they lack access to windows or boredom. I guess Theodore just prefers watching real birds from the window to Animal Planet.

14) Do Cats Listen To Music?

Some owners turn on the radio for their cats when they are away the whole day. Cats in general seem to like music. Some shelters even play classical music because of its calming effects.
I have not discovered which genre Theodore prefers, but so far he has not objected to my choice of music. Maybe he has good taste in music like his mama.

15) Coat Colors And Patterns of Cats

People sometimes confuse tabby, tortoiseshell and calico as a cat breed. But actually they refer to the color and pattern of the cats. For e.g. a calico coloration can occur on a British Shorthair, Persian or Siberian.

- **Solid** means a coat of one color e.g. black, blue (bluish-gray) and white.

- **Bicolor** means a coat of white plus one other color (either solid or a tabby pattern). A Tuxedo is a black cat with white face, belly and paws.

- **Tabby** is the most common coat pattern with an "M" marking on the forehead and a black "eyeliner" appearance. Tabby originated from the African wild cat.

There are four types of tabby:

- Mackerel (striped or fishbone) tabby pattern is the most common. It has narrow vertical stripes on the side of the body, tail and legs. These stripes can be solid or broken into spots or bars on the flanks and stomach. The belly also has a double row of "vest buttons". They are known as mackerel tabbies because of the parallel markings resembling fish bones on their sides, shoulder and haunches.

- Classic tabby (blotched or marbled) tends to have colors of dark browns, ocher, black and gray. Their body's side markings have large swirls or blotches resembling a bullseye ending in a circular pattern.

- Ticked tabby's (stripe-less) do not have the usual stripes, blotches or swirls but agouti hairs (light and dark colored bands) which produce a salt and pepper or sand-like patterns. They carry the typical "M" marking on their foreheads.

- Spotted tabby's have dark blotches of oval or round spots. They might also have a faint trace of "necklace".

Theodore is a typical silver mackerel tabby. I like to call his tail a "raccoon tail" because of the dark bandings around it.

Tortoiseshell (or torties) comes in a mix of black (smoky coal, chocolate brown, slivery gray or blue) and orange forming an unique coat pattern.

Calico (or tricolor) comes in white, black and orange (red) coat pattern.

Do You Know?

Most calico and tortoiseshell cats are females. This is due to a combination of genes, XX and XY chromosomes. It is estimated only 1 in 3000 is a male Calico and being XXY means they are normally sterile.

The ever popular Japanese Maneki-Neko lucky figurine is a Calico cat with an upright paw. It is often displayed in shops and restaurants and normally at the cash register.

Ginger cats (orange color or orange and white color, with or without tabby patterns) tends to be 75% males. Winston Churchill had a beloved ginger tabby named Jock who attended cabinet meetings during World War II, and even joined them for meals. Garfield is an orange tabby.

How Tabbies Got The "M" Marking On Their Foreheads

Once upon a time, there was a baby named J crying nonstop because of the frigid cold in the manger. His mother Mary did not know what to do despite bundling baby J in layers of cloth. A tabby cat was awoken from his nap and curiously went to see the commotion. Upon seeing the situation, the clever cat curled up next to baby J thus keeping him toasty and sleeping peacefully. Mary gratefully petted the helpful cat on his head and drew her initial "M" so that all would know the kind deed and remember to be kind to one another.

Epilogue

I have a secret to tell you. I was not named after the famous US President Theodore Roosevelt, like my mama tells people. But after her favorite TV cartoon chipmunk. This explains my bottomless stomach and ferocious appetite. Often I summon my bleary-eyed mama out of bed to feed me at unearthly hours. Frankly, I still don't get why 5am is unearthly to some hoomans. Anyway I can't sleep when I'm hungry and I need my beauty sleep a lot.

My mama wonders where I came from and what my life was like before she adopted me. But all that is distant memory to me now. The present moment is what matters. Why do hoomans like to dwell on the past and worry about the future so much? In my humble opinion, they'll be much happier if they learn to be more present like us. We just eat, sleep, play - repeat. Be here now, be there later. Easy peasy right?

Right now I'm just focused on being the center of her universe by hijacking her favorite chair or lying strategically across her keyboard as she tries her best to type out these sentences error free.

When I feel loving, I will show my love by looking vaguely in her direction and say nothing. Did I mention subtle is my middle name?

xo ~Theodore

P.S. Do you like the handsome picture of me on the cover?

P.P.S. You will be happy to know by purchasing this book; you are also contributing to our local animal. Therefore, if you've enjoyed this book –you can pay it forward by giving a supportive review on my mommy's book. Your kind review will help promote this book and channel more proceeds towards animals in need. Thank you very much for your compassion towards other animals. You can leave your review here: **http://www.amazon.com/review/create-review?&asin= B074L1H3T7**

Check Out My Other Books

Read about Theodore and his sister Julia here....

https://www.amazon.com/gp/product/B095DGV6WD

Printed in Great Britain
by Amazon